STOP WAITING
FOR PERMISSION
STUDY GUIDE

STOP WAITING FOR PERMISSION STUDY GUIDE

Harness Your Gifts,
Find Your Purpose, and
Unleash Your Personal Genius

STEPHEN CHANDLER

WATERBROOK

Published in the United States by WaterBrook, an imprint of Random House, a division of Penguin Random House LLC.

WATERBROOK® and its deer colophon are registered trademarks of Penguin Random House LLC.

Portions of this work originally appeared in *Stop Waiting for Permission* by Stephen Chandler, published in the United States by WaterBrook, an imprint of Random House, a division of Penguin Random House LLC in 2022.

Library of Congress Cataloging-in-Publication Data
Names: Chandler, Stephen, author.
Title: Stop waiting for permission study guide: harness your gifts, find your purpose, and unleash your personal genius / Stephen Chandler.
Description: First edition. | Colorado Springs: WaterBrook, [2022]
Identifiers: LCCN 2022015090 | ISBN 9780593194263 (paperback) | ISBN 9780593194270 (ebook)
Subjects: LCSH: Chandler, Stephen, Stop waiting for permission. | Self-actualization (Psychology)—Religious aspects—Christianity—Textbooks.
Classification: LCC BV4598.2 .C433 2022 | DDC 158.1—dc23/eng/20220407
LC record available at https://lccn.loc.gov/2022015090

Printed in the United States of America on acid-free paper

waterbrookmultnomah.com

2 4 6 8 9 7 5 3 1

First Edition

Book design by Diane Hobbing

SPECIAL SALES Most WaterBrook books are available at special quantity discounts when purchased in bulk by corporations, organizations, and special-interest groups. Custom imprinting or excerpting can also be done to fit special needs. For information, please email specialmarketscms@penguinrandomhouse.com.

CONTENTS

INTRODUCTION

I believe with all my heart that God designed you for a purpose and filled you with potential. I also believe that by living your purpose and working to realize your potential, you can attain greatness. I wrote my book, *Stop Waiting for Permission,* to inspire people like you to reach for your God-given greatness.

As much as I enjoy inspiring people, however, I want more: I want you to actually *become great*! This guide is designed to take you step by step through a process of soaking in God's Word, reflecting on your pursuit of greatness, and living into the principles of *Stop Waiting for Permission.* I wrote it with you in mind, in prayerful hope that you'll be intentional about setting aside time, mental energy, and spiritual space to begin your journey toward greatness.

You *can* work through my book and this guide on your own, but just like the quest for greatness itself, it's work that is best done in good, godly company. Whether it's with your significant other, a family member, a couple of close friends, or a book group, you'll find that dialogue, feedback, and encouragement from others—not to mention their prayers—will amplify your efforts. I recommend reading each chapter of *Stop Waiting for Permission* on your own, working through the corresponding session in this guide either on your own or with another person, and then coming together to share what you're discovering along the way.

Don't rush through it. I truly believe that prayerful, thoughtful, intentional engagement with the process I've laid out here will launch you toward the purpose you were created for. I can't wait to see what our great God does in, for, and through you!

HOW TO USE THIS GUIDE

This guide is a companion to the book *Stop Waiting for Permission,* and it can be used individually or in book clubs, discussion gatherings, and other kinds of small groups. Using this guide alongside the book will help you (and your group, if you're part of a discussion group) to get the most out of this content.

This guide consists of ten study sessions, and each session can be completed in a week, as is common for small groups. However, if you prefer to work through this guide on your own, you can certainly take the journey at your own pace.

READING SCHEDULE FOR *STOP WAITING FOR PERMISSION*

If you haven't already read the book *Stop Waiting for Permission,* do so as you work your way through these sessions. The book chapters flow with the sessions. So you'll read chapter 1 before session 1, chapter 2 before session 2, and so on, ending with chapter 10 and session 10 (there isn't a session for chapter 11).

Session Format

Every session will begin with a brief introduction (or re-introduction, if you've already read the book) to the topic for that session.

Soak It In

Read the biblical passage referenced in this section in the Bible translation of your choice. Then try reading the same passage in at least one additional version such as The Living Bible or the New King James Version. You can access multiple versions online or through an app such as YouVersion.

Each time you do this, first read the passage silently, then read it aloud a second time, and if you feel so inclined, rewrite it in your journal. Sometimes repeating a passage and then writing it down can help you retain it. Once you've read the passage and thought about it, respond to the questions or prompts that follow.

Reflect on It

The deeper questions in this section will encourage you (and your group) to dive into the core theme of the session in a way that might stimulate further thought and discussion.

Live into It

Every session will give you space to start thinking about how to apply the lessons to your life. This section might include an activity, questions to consider, or prompts to do something about what you learned.

Pray It Out

Every session will end with a prayer that you can read and pray individually or with your small group.

LEADING A SMALL GROUP DISCUSSION

If you're working through this study in a group setting and you're the facilitator of your group, here are some simple guidelines that can help make this ten-week journey through *Stop Waiting for Permission* more rewarding. Each session has enough content for sixty to ninety minutes of group time, depending on how long your group likes to spend in deeper discussion of each topic, Scripture passage, question, and application.

If you're part of an established small group going through *Stop Waiting for Permission,* your group is probably familiar with how to review content in studies like this one. It may not be necessary to prescribe every detail of the meetings, though this brief refresher may help you prepare for the discussions.

Review & Pray

Before meeting with the group, read the chapter of *Stop Waiting for Permission* associated with the study session (read chapter 1 before session 1, chapter 2 before session 2, etc.) and complete the session in this study guide. Then pray for each person in your group and for your upcoming time together.

Group Members

Encourage every group member to read the assigned chapter of *Stop Waiting for Permission* and complete the session in this guide before the meeting each week.

Getting Started & Introduction

Once your group members have arrived, take a few minutes to settle into a place free of distractions, where you can sit comfortably for sixty to ninety minutes. Then, when you're ready to get started, ask a group member to read the session's introduction aloud.

Soak It In

Ask someone else to read the Scripture passage named in this section of the study session, then ask each person to share the initial thoughts they wrote down or anything that came to mind as the passage was read aloud.

Reflect on It

Encourage discussion of the questions in this section, and remember to take your time. Don't rush the answers. Try to make sure no one person answers every question or dominates the discussion, and seek to get everyone involved, if you can. If someone isn't actively participating, try to draw them into the discussion gently. If you can create a safe space for honest reflection and discussion, your group time (and relationships with one another) will be more valuable.

Live into It & Pray It Out

Give the group time to talk about what they each wrote in the application section and to share ideas about how to apply what they've learned to their daily lives. Pray together to close your time.

STOP WAITING
FOR PERMISSION
STUDY GUIDE

SESSION 1

Why You Should Want Greatness

BASED ON CHAPTER 1 OF
STOP WAITING FOR PERMISSION

TAKEAWAY:
WHEN IT COMES TO GREATNESS,
YOU DON'T HAVE TO WAIT FOR
PERMISSION.

When it comes to greatness, too many people are just waiting to get lucky. They stand around day after day in the proverbial waiting room in the hope that someone else will fail to show up and forfeit their position inside.

Why would you do that when you can reserve your own place of greatness? There *will* be a seat at the table with your name on it, if you only call ahead and give your name. I want to show you how to prepare your life for the greatness God has planned for you.

You may have already accomplished some things other people consider great. They're impressed. Your influence is wide, your responsibilities are significant, and your list of accolades is long—but you still feel unfulfilled. You find yourself standing around, wondering, *Is this it? Is this all there is?* If that's you, I want to show you how to orient your drive and gifts toward the deeper purposes of God, where true greatness awaits.

Soak It In

Read Matthew 20:17–28 at least twice through, aloud if possible, from at least two Bible translations.

Spend a minute or two thinking about the passage. Who stands out to you? What are they doing or saying that captures your attention? Why do you find that interesting? Write and/or talk about what you notice.

Reflect on It

1. When you read about James and John asking to be great, how do you feel about their ambition? Why do you feel that way?

2. In Matthew 20, do you identify more with James and John or with the other disciples? What do you imagine you'd be feeling if you were in their place? Why?

3. Many things can hold people back from realizing their potential for greatness. From the list below, check the limitations you resonate with most:

   ☐ They're full of potential but short on drive.

   ☐ They're driven but lack direction.

   ☐ They're paralyzed into inaction by fear and doubt.

   ☐ They don't believe they deserve greatness.

   ☐ They don't see room for themselves or someone like them among those who are great.

   Where do you think those limitations come from?

What feelings, beliefs, or attitudes would you add to the list?

4. God has hidden greatness inside you. Your job is to knock down walls of fear, insecurity, and false humility to reveal what He has placed in you. When we search out what God has hidden, we increase our influence and fulfillment—our glory.

Proverbs 25:2 says, "It is the glory of God to conceal a matter; to search out a matter is the glory of kings." Is it fairly easy or difficult to think of yourself as royalty? Why?

Imagine what it would look like to treat your pursuit of godly greatness as a royal quest. How would thinking of it that way change your overall mindset?

Live into It

There is a place where everything that makes you who you are is welcomed and celebrated, where your gifts, passion, and purpose collide to leave a mark beyond your wildest imagining. In this place, you experience fulfillment by using your unique personal genius—yes, it exists!—to bless your family, friends, community, and world.

Use your holy imagination to begin envisioning this reality. In your place of greatness, how do you spend your time? Where are you? Who is with you? What kind of challenges do you face? What feelings do you experience most often? Why?

Take your time, and consider these questions for a few minutes, hours, or even days. Write about or sketch your place of greatness in the space below. Share your musings with one or two others.

Pray It Out

Great God, I believe You're calling me to greatness.
Or at least, I want to believe it.
I'm not sure yet what true greatness looks like,
but I will follow where You lead.
Help me respond in faith, not fear,
and dare to dream Your dreams for my life.
I want to please You and
bring You glory and honor in everything I do.
Amen.

SESSION 2

No Excuses Allowed

BASED ON CHAPTER 2 OF
STOP WAITING FOR PERMISSION

TAKEAWAY:
PUSH THROUGH YOUR FEARS, AND
LET YOUR LIMITATIONS LIBERATE
YOU FROM SMALL THINKING, SMALL
HOPES, AND SMALL FAITH.

When we're uncertain of our abilities or don't like the hand we've been dealt, some of us raise the bar of greatness so high that we start to feel okay about not reaching for it at all.

Who says you're not a great parent unless your child speaks three languages, plays four sports, and never comes in second place?

Who claims you've failed as an entrepreneur if your organization doesn't turn a profit within three months?

Who insists that a degree you earn in five years while working to support your family is worth less than a degree earned in four?

Who maintains that memorizing Scripture is pointless unless you learn entire books or that prayer counts as holy only if clocked by the hour?

Who says your efforts to eat healthier and move more are completely useless if you decide not to train for the New York City Marathon?

Nobody.

Don't allow what-ifs to become excuses.

Maybe it's hard to imagine being debt-free and having money above and beyond what you need, enough that you can pay off someone else's student loans. Fair enough, but you *can* make one wiser financial choice today.

Maybe it's hard to imagine your marriage becoming a union that deepens in love and trust each year. Okay, but you *can* make it a little more loving and trusting right now.

Don't use imagined impossibilities as excuses.

Soak It In

Read Matthew 25:14–30 at least twice through, aloud if possible, from at least two Bible translations.

Spend a minute or two thinking about the passage. Who stands out to you? What are they doing or saying that captures your attention? Why do you find that interesting? Write and/or talk about what you notice.

Reflect on It

1. Just like it did to the one-talent manager, fear of failure can paralyze us into inaction. Here's the thing, though: Fear of failure is often vague. Try to get specific.

   What exactly are you afraid of when it comes to your quest for greatness?

What is the worst outcome that you can imagine?

Now be honest with yourself: How likely is it to happen?

2. Unrealistic expectations are more often a figment of our imaginations than an accurate assessment of reality. By obsessing over our limitations and lack of resources, we distort our understanding of what God wants for us.

What do you believe God expects of you?

How does that compare with what you think He expects of others?

How do you think the time you spend observing other people, either on social media or in person, affects your perception of yourself?

Is this a help or a hindrance to your pursuit of greatness? Why?

3. With more limitations, there's a smaller margin for error. But remember, those disadvantages can be an incredibly powerful driver of creativity.

   In the first column below, list what you think of as your main disadvantages, whether financial, physical, social, educational, or otherwise.

Disadvantage	→	Creativity
_____	→	_____
_____	→	_____
_____	→	_____
_____	→	_____
_____	→	_____
_____	→	_____
_____	→	_____
_____	→	_____
_____	→	_____
_____	→	_____

Now go back and look at your list. Think of those constraints as jumping-off places for creative thinking and innovative problem-solving. In the second column, write down how successfully navigating each limitation might take you further on your journey to greatness. If you get stuck, ask for input from someone who knows you well.

4. You're in proximity to people with resources you lack and ideas you can't imagine. Asking for help can activate your progress toward greatness. Make a list of people in your life or network who might be able to help you with resources or ideas.

Formulate a plan to reach out to them in the coming week.

Live into It

I know without a shadow of a doubt that there is greatness in you—yes, *you*—entrusted to you by our Creator. The treasure He has placed in your keeping has the potential to multiply everything you invest in. But in order to see a return, you must . . .

1. **Allow God to heal your heart.** What are the hurts and disappointments that cloud the eyes of your heart? Spend as much time as needed to lay them at His feet. You may need to process them with a trusted friend or wise counselor.

2. **Celebrate every win.** Where are you investing your potential well, even in very small ways?

You're a great manager of what God has invested in you! Take time to celebrate these small wins with the people around you.

3. **Overcome your fear of failure.** The best way to overcome fear is to do it anyway, so start investing in
   what God has placed in you. Make a list of the small
   investments you'll make today, this week, this month.
   Be specific for each area of your life in which you're
   pursuing greatness.

Pray It Out

Great God, I need Your help and healing.
Wounds and failures in my past are
weighing me down and keeping me from
the future You've planned for me.
Please use the adversities I've faced
to strengthen me for this pursuit of greatness.
Show me how to invest the potential
You've deposited in me
and to celebrate every success with You.
I know You will never leave or forsake me,
and I'm thankful.
Amen.

Fuel for the Road Trip
to Greatness

BASED ON CHAPTER 3 OF
STOP WAITING FOR PERMISSION

TAKEAWAY:
THE RIGHT MOTIVATIONS COULD BE
THE MOST IMPORTANT FACTOR OF
YOUR JOURNEY TO GREATNESS.

There is no direct flight to greatness. It's a road trip. The journey is always by land, and stops to fuel up are mandatory, whether your vehicle runs on gas, electricity, biodiesel, or whatever. It requires perseverance, a reliable map, and, if you're on the road with others, patience and a sense of humor.

Don't get me wrong, though. It doesn't have to be miserable. Even the stops can be refreshing—depending on where you stop for fuel and what you put in the tank. We are all fueled by something. And what fuels you matters.

Here's a thought that sometimes keeps me up at night: The wrong fuel can offer breakneck progress in the short term. I mean, fill up your gas tank with rocket fuel, and you'll get *somewhere* very, very fast—it just may not be where you want to go, and you likely won't be in one piece when you get there.

No one but Jesus is perfect, of course, but people fueled up and firing on all cylinders take my breath away. Instead of burning up on the first leg of the trip, they can sustain life on the road day after day, year after year. Their fuel is clean, efficient, and powerful.

Soak It In

Read Galatians 1:10–16; 2:4–7, 19–21 at least twice through, aloud if possible, from at least two Bible translations.

Spend a minute or two thinking about the passage. When you think about Paul's conversion and his calling from Jesus, what does he seem to have been most passionate about? How do you think Paul would have described his purpose? Write and/or talk about your thoughts.

Reflect on It

1. Write one or two sentences below describing your passion(s). Not sure what you're passionate about? Here are some questions to help you get started: What can you talk about for hours without running out of things to say? What demands your attention every time it crosses your path, igniting your instincts to go after it and make it your own?

How does your passion(s) connect to different areas of your life, whether social, professional, spiritual, or otherwise?

What can you do to keep the fire ablaze?

2. In his book *Wishful Thinking*, theologian and writer Frederick Buechner wrote that purpose "is the place where your deep gladness and the world's deep hunger meet." Spend some time thinking, praying, and talking or writing about the needs you see around you.

How could your passion(s) intersect with the needs of others and bless them?

3. Which wrong fuels are you likely to fill up with? Fear? Pride? Comparison? In the first column, list the fuels you're driven by. In the second column, record your feelings and behaviors when you're running on those fuels (i.e., Do you isolate from others? Do you pretend to be someone you're not? Do you sleep or eat too much or too little?).

When I fill up with	→	I feel/act
_____	→	_____
_____	→	_____
_____	→	_____
_____	→	_____
_____	→	_____
_____	→	_____
_____	→	_____
_____	→	_____
_____	→	_____
_____	→	_____
_____	→	_____

Make a plan for what you'll do when you notice these feelings and behaviors.

Talk with a trusted friend this week about helping each other keep away from the wrong fuels.

Live into It

When eternity is your fuel, your road trip to greatness keeps going and going and going and going. No matter what you spend your days doing, your life can be fueled by eternity.

In the space on the next page, write down three to five of your day-to-day activities. Then write a short prayer next to each activity. In the coming week, pray that prayer every time you do that activity.

For example, if parenting young children is a big part of each day, you might write something like "Dear heavenly Father, help me love and guide these kids with patience and wisdom, and help me point them to You. Amen." Then say that prayer every time you're "on duty."

After a few days of praying that your activities would resonate in eternity, what do you notice? How is your view of yourself, others, and God shifting or staying the same?

Pray It Out

*Great God, I want my
motivations to honor You.
Make me more like Your Son, Jesus.
Calm my fears.
Draw my attention away from myself.
Stop unhelpful comparison in its tracks.
Convert the engine of my life
to run on life-giving fuels.
Increase my passion for what You love.
Reveal Your purpose for my life.
Keep me oriented toward eternity.
Realign my motivations with Yours.
Amen.*

SESSION 4

The Key to Unlock Your Purpose

BASED ON CHAPTER 4 OF
STOP WAITING FOR PERMISSION

TAKEAWAY:
YOUR UNIQUE GENIUS IS THE KEY
THAT UNLOCKS GREATNESS.

No matter where I am or what I'm supposed to be doing, I want to find out why something works well and what people do to make it happen consistently. I'm a little ashamed to admit it, but I've taken my wife out for dinner and found myself chatting with the general manager about how he selects and trains high-caliber staff and with the chef about building her award-winning menu. I don't *need* to know, but I can't help myself! I can't turn my genius off, even in situations that have nothing to do with my own passion and purpose. It operates whether I want it to or not. Where do you see this happening for you?

When you walk into a room, what do you notice first? Is it the people—their body language, facial expressions, and tone of voice—or is it how well or poorly they're completing their tasks? If it's the people who demand your attention, what stands out to you? Do you notice group dynamics? How people speak over the music and one another? Or do you focus on the one or two individuals who don't appear to be enjoying themselves? Or the couple in the corner who are having a whispered disagreement?

If you notice the quality of work first, observe what holds your attention. Are you imagining a more artistic or compelling way to present what's being shared, marveling over the seamless execution, or cringing because just one part of the whole isn't up to snuff?

Every room you walk into can bring your genius out, if you'll only take notice. Pay attention, and let your key find you.

Soak It In

Read Psalm 139:1–18 at least twice through, aloud if possible, from at least two Bible translations.

Spend a minute or two thinking about the passage. Which ideas or images do you find most reassuring? And which do you find most challenging or difficult to believe? Write and/or talk about why you respond in that way.

Reflect on It

1. God used extreme care when He created you, making you distinct from anyone else before or since. What would your journey to greatness look like if you fully believed that?

How would that belief influence your passion and purpose?

Memorize some of Psalm 139, and pray those verses at different times throughout the day. After a few days of this practice, what do you notice?

Choose one or two people in your life who need to hear this message. Encourage them this week by reminding them of their uniqueness. How did it affect their week?

2. Genius is a God-given advantage that sets someone apart from the pack. Think about one or two people you deeply admire. How would you describe their genius?

Why do you think it's easier to recognize genius in others?

3. It's easy to get hung up on areas of genius that God *didn't* give you. Part of the journey is developing enough self-awareness to walk away from wishful thinking. What's an area of genius that you wish you had?

How might it influence your journey to greatness if you divert attention away from that area and instead focus on the genius God has given you?

4. It's time to find your genius so you can unlock all the horsepower of your purpose and race toward the greatness God has destined for you.

In the space below, make a list of all your abilities. If you need a little extra help, review the questions under "Where to Look and What to Look For" (pages 62–66) in the book.

Choose one or two trusted people who know you well. Ask them for input on your list. What would they add to it?

Live into It

Your genius is the key to your purpose. It connects you more deeply to God, others, and yourself. Genius is others-directed. That's what sets it apart from your other talents. How are you using your genius to serve your God-given purpose? What could you do differently to focus your genius toward your purpose?

Pray It Out

Great God, show me the genius
You've placed inside me so I can accomplish my purpose.
Help me not get distracted by gifts I don't have
but instead trust that You know what You're doing.
Teach me to enjoy the process of self-discovery
and to be patient for all the good
You're working on my behalf.
Direct me to people and situations that
need my genius, and show me how to help.
Amen.

All Four Wheels Ready to Roll

BASED ON CHAPTER 5 OF
STOP WAITING FOR PERMISSION

TAKEAWAY:
GREATNESS IS BUILT ON A FIRM
FOUNDATION. TAKE THE TIME TO
ESTABLISH A FOUNDATION THAT
WILL LAST.

The opening scene of the animated movie *Cars* haunts me. The rookie upstart, Lightning McQueen, is in the final race of his first season in pursuit of the Piston Cup. He's racing against the beloved champion, Strip Weathers, and the perpetual runner-up, Chick Hicks. Lightning's driving is balletic, almost otherworldly, and soon he's at the front of the pack with a commanding lead. It's his race to lose.

Then he makes a fatal mistake. While all the other cars head into the pits for fuel and tires, he hits the gas the second his tank is full, refusing to wait for a fresh set of wheels. He's determined to keep his lead, even though his tires are wearing thinner with each lap.

Throughout the second half of the race, it looks like Lightning's roll of the dice is going to pay off . . . until the final turn.

He blows a tire. The crowd gasps! But he's so far out in front of his nearest competitors that he might win anyway, limping along on three worn-out tires. He keeps the pedal to the metal and aims for the checkered flag, fishtailing his way toward the finish line.

Then he blows another tire.

Like the tires that Lightning McQueen needed to win the race, there are four "wheels" that are absolutely crucial for our race to greatness. None of them is optional; each is essential. If you and I want to show up on time to our appointment with destiny, we must prioritize these four aspects of character: vision, faithfulness, self-discipline, and balance.

Soak It In

Read 1 Chronicles 28 through 2 Chronicles 1:13 at least twice through, aloud if possible, from at least two Bible translations. It's a long passage, but your pursuit of greatness is worth investing in!

Spend a minute or two thinking about the story. Who stands out to you? What are they doing or saying that captures your attention? Why do you find that interesting? Write and/or talk about what you notice.

Reflect on It

1. Review the four aspects of character in chapter 5. Through what actions or attitudes did David and Solomon demonstrate each of these character traits in the passage you read earlier in this session?

2. Now it's your turn to cultivate the four aspects of character so you can go the distance on the road to greatness.

Vision

Vision grows from the habit of asking and answering the right questions for each area of your life in which you want to pursue greatness. Choose one or two areas in which you're pursuing greatness, and work through the questions below:

• Where am I?

• Where am I headed?

• Where do I want to go?

• How do I get from here to there?

• What resources and companions do I need to get there?

• What will I do along the way?

• Where will I *not* be able to go? (And am I at peace with that?)

Faithfulness

Why is faithfully showing up such an important part of the journey to greatness?

How are you doing when it comes to faithfully showing up?

Thinking about the one or two areas in which you're pursuing greatness, sketch out at least three SBAGs, "Stretching but Achievable Goals," to use as a jumping-off place to start new habits of faithfulness. (Refer back to page 78 in the book for a refresher on SBAGs.)

Self-Discipline

Assess yourself in the three areas of self-discipline:

1. Keeping track of your commitments
2. Managing your time
3. Attending to details

Circle the area in which you're strongest.

Put a square around the area in which you're weakest.

Draw a star next to the area that will be your priority to improve this week.

What specific action(s) will you take to improve the area you identified?

Balance

Look at the various components of life listed below. Use the extra lines to include any other areas in which you'd like to pursue greatness. Once you've compiled your full list, rate your level of stability in each area, with 1 being the least stable and 5 being the most stable.

Component of life   →   Level of stability

Mental _____ → _____

Emotional _____ → _____

Spiritual _____ → _____

Relational _____ → _____

Financial _____ → _____

Rest _____ → _____

_____ → _____

_____ → _____

_____ → _____

_____ → _____

What do you notice about your list? Are there areas where you're succeeding? Lacking?

Live into It

Where does developing spiritual greatness rank among your priorities? Do you feel confident that you have the spiritual resources to deal well with greatness in other areas of your life? Where do you need to increase your reserves, and what action(s) will you take to do it?

Pray It Out

Great God, blessing and favor are
Yours to give, and I know I can't earn them.
But I also know I have work to do
to become who You created me to be.
Please give me the determination
and tenacity to develop vision,
faithfulness, self-discipline, and balance.
Show me where I'm falling short
of my potential, and guide my efforts
so they bear fruit that honors You.
Amen.

Become an Aggressive

Apprentice

BASED ON CHAPTER 6 OF
STOP WAITING FOR PERMISSION

TAKEAWAY:
CHOOSING THE RIGHT COACH CAN
MAKE ALL THE DIFFERENCE.

No one likes a bully. (Jesus loves bullies, but not even He has to *like* them.) And because no one likes a bully, aggression gets a bad rap. It's often associated with the use of force, intimidation, and hostility.

But there's a subtly different understanding of aggression that turns it from something to be avoided into something to be (wisely) pursued. Aggression is *a readiness to confront or attack*. I want to suggest that when it's directed at our own ignorance and shortcomings, aggression can be a gift. When we don't live in denial about where we fall short, we're ready and willing to confront these areas and, with the Spirit's help, whip them into shape. We're relentless about learning more and doing better.

Once you start pursuing greatness, it's only a matter of time until you realize you're in over your head. Our visions are not ours to accomplish but God's to exceed. He does "immeasurably more than all we ask or imagine" (Ephesians 3:20)—and if that's true, we've got to get aggressive about learning. The good news is, what God has for you is so much bigger than you can imagine. The bad news is, what God has for you is so much bigger than the current *you* can manage.

Get even a glimmer of that destiny, and you'll feel a deep sense of urgency to start becoming the you who *can* manage it. When you start feeling that way, find the right teachers and become an apprentice—and don't take no for an answer.

Soak It In

Read 2 Kings 2 at least twice through, aloud if possible, from at least two Bible translations.

Spend a minute or two thinking about the story. Who stands out to you? What are they doing or saying that captures your attention? Why do you find that interesting? Write and/or talk about what you notice.

Reflect on It

1. When it came to reaching for greatness, Elisha wasn't afraid to ask for help. In what area of your life do you avoid asking for help or guidance?

Why do you think that area is such a challenge for you?

How can the right motivations help you take the posture of a learner?

2. List three or four people whose greatness you respect. Next to each name, write what it is about them that inspires you.

Without falling into mimicry, what can you learn from them and apply to your own pursuit of greatness?

3. What process do you depend on to choose reliable teachers?

How do you know whom to trust?

4. Be on the lookout for repeatable processes that produce consistent progress. A system is a step-by-step process that consistently results in the desired outcome with little or no variance. Since repeatability is a matter of reassessment and refinement, spend some time analyzing what's working and what's not in your pursuit of greatness.

What's working	What's not working

Why do you think the things you listed in the first column are going well?

How can you repeat that success?

Live into It

To create a system with repeatable results, you need to build in checkpoints. Moments where you, your partner, and/or your team can regularly reassess how the journey is going.

How does the idea of continual self-assessment feel to you? Exciting? Intimidating? Exhausting? Be honest with yourself about your desire to tackle or avoid it. Where do you think those feelings come from?

Using the vision you laid out in session 5, come up with a revisable plan of assessment.

Here are some questions to consider: How often will you pause to take stock of your progress, of what's working and what's not? What metrics will you use to evaluate your success? Who in your life can give wise input on your plan?

Pray It Out

Great God, I need to know
more to achieve my vision.
I want to be relentless
about learning and improving.
Keep me in a learning posture,
and give me courage to confront
my ignorance and shortcomings.
Make me humble and teachable, and
guide me to the teachers who can help me
master the purpose You've called me to.
Make me into the me who can
imagine and manage everything
You have for me.
Amen.

Too Big to Do Alone

BASED ON CHAPTER 7 OF
STOP WAITING FOR PERMISSION

TAKEAWAY:
A GREAT TEAM IS FUNDAMENTAL
TO YOUR PURSUIT OF GREATNESS.

Behind every championship and alongside every superstar athlete is a team that makes greatness possible. Teammates shoulder their part of the work, pick up one another's slack, and work together to bring home the win. Even in solo sports like singles tennis, car racing, golf, and boxing, there are teams of coaches, mechanics, caddies, and cutmen that ensure the star can perform at their highest potential.

A great team is fundamental to your pursuit of greatness even if you're a superstar solo athlete. Look at Jesus. He spent just three short years in ministry here on earth, and a hugely significant chunk of His time was spent building the team that would become the foundation of the global church. Like Him, we must spend significant time, effort, and focus on building a team. Why? Because even with all the unique genius, solid character, and holy motivation in the world, you are still only one person. Jesus was literally superhuman, which may mean He could have done without a team—but He didn't. To state the obvious, we aren't superhuman. Best to follow His example.

If you're going it alone and making progress, it may be tempting to think you can go all the way on your own. *A team is so much hassle,* you might think. *I can't guarantee anyone's work but my own. Maybe I'm better off by myself.* It's true that going it alone can be easier sometimes. But don't let easy trick you out of great. Build toward your vision before you have a team, but from day one, keep your eyes open for the right people to multiply your efforts.

My favorite verse of Scripture is Jeremiah 29:11: "'I know the plans I have for you,' declares the LORD, 'plans to prosper you and not to harm you, plans to give you hope and a future.'" If anyone has the right to be self-centered and use everyone else for His own agenda, it's God; He's the one who created us all in the first place! Yet here He says that He's thinking about *us*, planning for *us*, positioning *us* to prosper and to be full of hope for an amazing future.

That's the kind of leader I want to be—a leader who, like Jesus, "did not come to be served, but to serve" (Mark 10:45). That's true greatness.

Soak It In

Read Romans 16:1–16 at least twice through, aloud if possible, from at least two Bible translations.

Spend a minute or two thinking about the passage. Did you know that the apostle Paul worked with so many people? Did you recognize any names? If so, where else in the Bible have you read about them? Write and/or talk about what you notice.

Reflect on It

1. Take a look at the people around you. How are they helping or hindering your pursuit of greatness?

What changes do you need from your teammates?

2. Purpose is what makes a game-changing team. We encounter a problem, though, when we try to lead from a place of insecurity. We no longer see people, only pieces on a chessboard. But purpose-filled people don't want to be used. Those who stay in such conditions won't be the ones who can accomplish the vision and won't fill the shared journey with joy.

How are you confidently releasing your team to succeed and exceed your expectations?

In what areas are you leading from insecurity or fear?

What action(s) will you take to adjust your posture so you can inspire and motivate others?

3. The job of coaches is to understand the game better than anyone else on the field. It's your job to put each person in the right position, where their genius can shine and their weakness won't matter because it's someone else's strength.

   In the areas of life where you're a leader, how do you understand your role? How well are you doing, and how might you improve?

   In the areas where you're a follower, how is your leader failing or succeeding in coaching in a life-giving way? How are you positioned where you can shine?

Live into It

When you erect a building, some materials are foundational, some are framing, some are finishes, and some are scaffolding. It's the same with people you ask to be part of your team. Take inventory of the people in your life. Which part(s) of your architectural structure does each one fit into?

Foundation	Framing
Finishing Touches	Scaffolding

After you've created your list, prayerfully consider whether each person is where they need to be to fulfill their purpose. If a change is in order, use the space below to plan how to make the most of the transition.

Pray It Out

*Great God, sometimes I feel
like I just want to go it alone,
but the vision You've given me
is too big for that.
Give me courage to ask others
to join me on this journey to greatness.
Help me to discern the people
whose purpose aligns with mine
and to instill in them a love for my vision.
Keep each of us hungry, humble, and smart,
and help us love You and one another
with all our hearts.
Amen.*

Wise Leaps of Faith

BASED ON CHAPTER 8 OF
STOP WAITING FOR PERMISSION

TAKEAWAY:
TAKING RISKS IS INEVITABLE, BUT
THE RIGHT APPROACH WILL ALL
BUT GUARANTEE YOUR SUCCESS.

Greatness can't be attained without taking risks. You can't avoid jeopardy. If greatness is your aim, you'll have to take some chances.

What is risk? It's an action with exponential potential for failure or success. It might be as small as a comment that could either greatly offend or break the ice and forge instant connection. It might be as big as investing a large sum of money to flip a fixer-upper; your investment might pay a massive return, or you might be saddled with property you don't want. If you're on the road to greatness, you won't have to go looking for risk. It will come looking for you. It will often come in the form of a decision to forge ahead or stay where you are and secure what you've gained.

I love solid foundations and repeatable systems, but foundations and systems exist not for their own sake but in service to something greater. Think about a car factory, which is basically a lot of smaller systems that make up a big system to turn raw materials—metal, glass, plastic, leather, and electronic components—into automobiles. Risks are a raw material, and without them, greatness is impossible.

Risks are essential. And there are ways to take them wisely.

Soak It In

Read 1 Samuel 14:1–23 at least twice through, aloud if possible, from at least two Bible translations.

Spend a minute or two thinking about the story. Who stands out to you? What are they doing or saying that captures your attention? Why do you find that interesting? Write and/or talk about what you notice.

Reflect on It

1. Most people have an instinctual attraction to one or the other end of the spectrum between caution and risk. Mark on the scale below where you're most comfortable.

Cautious			Impulsive

2. What positive results have you seen from acting from your sweet spot on the scale above?

What negative results have you seen?

3. Now it's your turn to take a confident leap of faith toward greatness with this formula: **wisdom + peace + godly counsel.**

Wisdom

Why do you think consistency is a key component of wisdom?

What is one action you can take this week to be more consistent in applying knowledge?

Peace

God's unexplainable peace comes through the discipline of prayer. If you aren't engaging in a daily practice of prayer, peace will remain elusive. Start with just five to ten minutes each day. Pray out loud if that helps you stay focused, or use the space below to "think with God" through the decisions that are weighing on your mind.

What changes did you see in a day? In a week?

Godly Counsel

Make a list of trustworthy people in your life who can give you godly counsel. If no one immediately comes to mind, spend some time "thinking with God" about which two or three mentors you can ask.

Why are they a good choice?

What about their lives inspires you to leap wisely?

Live into It

Take a moment to reread the section titled "Betting the Farm . . . Wisely" (pages 134–137) in the book. Think about the following questions; then use the space below to write a paragraph that answers them:

- Which scenario is closer to where you find yourself on your journey to greatness—starting out or further along?
- How are you managing the tension between caution and risk?
- Which part of the formula do you need more of—wisdom, peace, or godly counsel? Where will you turn to get what you need to make a wise leap of faith?

Pray It Out

Great God, teach me
how to take wise leaps of faith.
I don't want to be too cautious or too impulsive.
I want to take risks in a way that pleases You.
Help me be consistent in practicing wisdom.
Give me Your unexplainable peace about the
decisions You want me to make.
Send godly counselors who will give good advice
and be willing to put skin in the game.
Make me willing to risk everything for You but
wise enough not to waste anything.
Amen.

No Pain, No Progress

BASED ON CHAPTER 9 OF
STOP WAITING FOR PERMISSION

TAKEAWAY:
DON'T BE SURPRISED BY PAIN, BUT
BE READY TO LEARN, HEAL, AND
PROGRESS THROUGH IT.

f we don't have the right mindset when pain comes, it's easy to fall into the trap of believing we're doing something wrong. (This was the trap Job's friends jumped into with both feet: "You must have secret sin in your life, or all these terrible things wouldn't be happening!") We might erroneously believe that if something's right, it should be easy, that God's blessing should always come without a fight.

But the apostle Paul took a different view. At its worst, pain for Paul was just par for the course. At its best, it was a badge of honor.

The book of Acts, written by Luke, details how serious Paul was: When he was stoned and dragged outside the city gates, his friends gathered around, fearing he was dead. But he revived, marched back into the city where he'd nearly been murdered, and picked up his ministry right where he left off (see 14:19–23). For Paul, getting stoned—not recreationally or medicinally, but with giant rocks thrown full-arm at his head—was just the price of doing gospel business.

Becoming a great parent, a great spouse, a great leader, or a great whatever will likely not include getting stoned nearly to death. But it's guaranteed to include some pain. I wish there were another way, but there isn't. Nothing worth doing comes easy.

I want to encourage you today to expect some pain in your life. If you're expecting it, you'll be more likely to keep yourself open to the lessons pain can teach you. Yes, I know it's not good to learn everything the hard way. When it's possible, take your lessons from other people's pain and hard experiences! But there are some lessons we just can't learn without some suffering to help them sink in.

Soak It In

Read James 1:2–18 at least twice through, aloud if possible, from at least two Bible translations.

Spend a minute or two thinking about the passage. What stands out to you? What does it mean to think of your trials and pain as "pure joy"? What would doing that look like? Write and/or talk about your thoughts.

Reflect on It

1. Pain is an unavoidable part of the journey to greatness. Do you agree? Why or why not?

What lessons have you learned through pain that you might not have learned otherwise?

2. Do you find it to be a consolation when you know the source of your pain? Why or why not?

When you consider any pain you're experiencing right now, are you able to identify where it's coming from? Spend some time writing and/or talking about your answer.

3. Much of the pain we humans experience is caused by other humans. We all make mistakes, and we're all in need of grace—including from ourselves!

Do you find it easier to forgive others or yourself? Are you more likely to blame yourself or let yourself off the hook?

Do you have trouble knowing the difference between extending grace and excusing bad behavior? Explain your answer.

Spend some time praying, writing, and/or talking about the people pain in your life. Where are you hurting most?

What action(s) can you take to set and maintain healthier boundaries?

4. How do you feel when the topic of spiritual warfare comes up? Why?

As you survey the landscape of your life, what area(s) do you see that may be spiritually undefended or less defended than they should be?

Which relationships in your life are unhealthy and leaving you open to spiritual attack?

Live into It

Think about a painful part of your life. Use the space below to reflect on it. Where are you hurting? What is the source of the pain?

Now come up with a plan to address it, because ignoring it will only make it worse. The longer you wait to face and embrace the discomfort, the more acute it will be. What will you do today to address it? What will you do this week? This month? Use the space below to detail a plan.

Pray It Out

Great God, thank You
for being present with me in pain.
Help me to be patient in seasons
of discomfort and to learn whatever
the pain can teach me about purpose,
greatness, myself, and You.
Guard my heart against the Enemy,
and heal relationships where pain
could open the door to spiritual attack.
Give me wisdom to discern the source of pain,
to respond with grace, and to choose You
no matter what the cost.
Amen.

A Price Not Worth Paying

BASED ON CHAPTER 10 OF
STOP WAITING FOR PERMISSION

TAKEAWAY:
PAYING THE RIGHT PRICE AND NOT
A PENNY MORE WILL ENSURE THAT
GREATNESS IS THE BLESSING GOD
DESIGNED IT TO BE.

As I'm writing, the world is slowly recovering from a global economic shutdown in response to the coronavirus pandemic that began in 2020. Global supply chains have broken down, wreaking havoc on nearly every industry—including construction, which has led to a shortage of new housing, which has led to skyrocketing prices for existing homes, which has led real estate investing nerds like me to push pause on new purchases. I refuse to catch buyer's fever and overpay for a house that in a few years will be worth less than I paid for it, giving me a severe case of buyer's remorse. A dream house becomes a nightmare when you owe more on it than you can sell it for.

You're probably thinking, *Wait—did this just turn into a real estate investing book?* No. But the principle that applies to the current housing market also applies to your pursuit of greatness: There's a price not worth paying. As bad as it is to be upside down on a mortgage, it's so much worse to be upside down on your life.

I wrote *Stop Waiting for Permission* to encourage you to invest in maximizing your potential and achieving greatness, but I also want to give you tools to do so in a godly, sustainable way. You're going to find such joy, fulfillment, and pleasure from discovering your genius and living your purpose! The problem is, the amazing opportunities you've prayed for will eventually ask more from you than is wise for you to give. Please trust me on this; I'm living it right now. I'm so grateful for every opportunity! But if I'm not intentional and careful, I'll find myself progressing toward greatness in one area but upside down on the rest of my life.

Soak It In

Read 2 Samuel 11 at least twice through, aloud if possible, from at least two Bible translations.

Spend a minute or two thinking about the story. Who stands out to you? What are they doing or saying that captures your attention? Why do you find that interesting? Write and/or talk about what you notice.

Reflect on It

1. David paid more for greatness than it was worth, and it cost him more than he could ever have imagined. When have you seen someone in your own life—a parent, a mentor, someone else you look up to—pay too great a price for their success?

2. Fear often drives us to pay more for greatness than it's worth. Step back and survey the areas where you're pursuing greatness.

   Where is fear prompting you to pay too great a price for success?

In what ways is your pursuit of greatness short-changing your spouse, children, friends, or health?

What will you do differently this week to bring your priorities back into alignment?

3. Sabbath is about living from a position of faith that God can accomplish more in our rest than we ever could in our pursuit. How does practicing Sabbath rest help you make your pursuit of greatness a pursuit of God?

If you're not practicing Sabbath rest, what is keeping you from it? Why?

If you are regularly practicing Sabbath rest, what does that look like for you? If not, what would it look like if you chose to practice Sabbath rest?

4. Take some significant time to evaluate the most important relationships in your life (e.g., your relationships with your spouse, your kids, and your closest friends). How do you feel about how you're prioritizing these relationships? What do you wish were different? What can *you* do to change the dynamic?

• *Relationship 1:*

- *Relationship 2:*

- *Relationship 3:*

Live into It

Is it easy or hard for you to relax? Why? How do you feel about the amount of time, energy, and resources you invest in recreation? What will you do this week to enjoy God's presence and spend time with Him?

Pray It Out

Great God, I want to make You smile.
Help me not be so focused on greatness
that I lose sight of You and all the
blessings that make life worth living.
Teach me how to pursue Your purpose
in all my relationships.
Lead me to re-create wholehearted joy
and to receive each of Your good gifts
with thanks and praise.
Help me be content in every situation
because I'm with You.
Amen.

"*Stop Waiting for Permission* is going to help you find the greatness within you. This book needs to be not in your library; it needs to be on your lap."

— JOHN MAXWELL, leadership expert, speaker, and *New York Times* bestselling author

Get your copy of *Stop Waiting for Permission* by Stephen Chandler. Your personal genius is waiting to be released!

Learn more at stephenrchandler.com/stopwaitingforpermission